How to Start A Micro-Distillery For Under $50,000

Thomas Germann

Copyright © 2013 Thomas Germann

All rights reserved.

ISBN: 148193483X
ISBN-13: 978-1481934831

DEDICATION

This book is dedicated to the men and women who serve or have served in the Armed Forces of the United States and my loving family who encouraged me each step of the way as I spent countless hours researching, developing and building my business. Without the support of so many good friends and caring people along the way, I'm not sure The Original Texas Legend Distillery would have come to fruition. You have blessed me by your word-of-mouth advertising, recommending our products and coming on my journey with me and I thank you.

-Thomas

Special thanks to my loving wife who was encouraging and supportive throughout my adventures and to my many wonderful friends for the support, networking and encouragement.

How to start a micro-distillery

Foreword:

Starting a micro-distillery is a lot of work but can be done for under $50,000 by the average person willing to put in the work and time to research carefully. This book will cover the topics and challenges I faced as I created The Original Texas Legend Distillery. The federal laws governing alcohol businesses are the same for all states, but state laws will vary from state to state. Research on the internet and blogs tell you it will cost approximately $250,000 to $500,000 to start a micro-distillery. However, searching for the best prices on the equipment, you can save a lot of money.

Before you begin, you will need to establish a business plan and make a lot of determinations. Chief among these is the type of business to establish. Is your business going to be owned by you alone, will you have a partner, or will you set your business up as a Corporation? Much of the information given in this book will be general or will be specific to my state, Texas. But the information contained should be applicable, in part, to where you're located and give clear guidelines where to start as research your own states' specific laws.

There are many reasons a person may want to start their own business. For me, it was a desire to be in control of my time, hours, income, and the satisfaction of owning my own business. I believe that practically anyone can form their own business, but there is an absence of information for this type of business. I hope this guide will provide some direction. The main criteria, I believe, a person needs to be successful in starting their own business is determination and perseverance. You will face countless roadblocks, encounter problems, and difficulties along the journey. Understand from the beginning things will happen. You must work through them while staying committed to your idea to ensure your success and the realization of your dream. If you have only a little knowledge on distilleries, distilling, networking or business, prepare yourself to do a lot of reading. The internet is a wonderful source of information so try searching blogs, newspaper and magazine articles and Internet forums. Get your hands on as much material as possible to read and educate yourself on ideas from others, solutions to problems others have discovered and gain a strong knowledge base.

Oftentimes, in joining newsgroups and forums, you will encounter people that have been there and done that and can answer your questions. In this book, I give my e-mail address and will be happy to hear from you, and assist as time allows me. I will tell you now, there is no way around doing your research. If you are not willing to put in the time to read and educate yourself so that you can solve your own problems as you encounter them, you will not be able to successfully launch your business by yourself or at the reduced costs mentioned in this book.

The majority of people who open distilleries, breweries or wineries have substantial amounts of money they spend on professionals to guide them, direct in their purchases, and educate them on the process of starting a business. With careful preparation, reading as much material as possible, and taking the time to shop around for the absolute best price on services and equipment, you can save HUGE sums of money.

Let's dig in…

CONTENTS

Chapter 1

Introduction

So you want to start a micro-distillery? The first thing that you're going to need will be money. I suggest you have between $15-$25,000 cash before you even begin. If you have the money on hand, the next thing you want to do is determine the structure of your business. It's very easy to go on the internet to look up the pros and cons of sole proprietorship, partnership, limited liability companies and corporations. I am not qualified to give legal advice, but I saved the money I could have spent on attorney fees by researching the small business administration's website and various other places to determine the type of business and the structure for what I was about to do.

In my state, business filings are done through the Secretary of State. I began with a web search on the Secretary of State website and found I could research how to create a business name and found the filing forms that were needed to establish my business. I chose a limited liability company as the business structure for my distillery because it provides some protection for me, as an owner, but still allows the flexibility for the company to change quickly as needed without having to have board meetings as a Corporation would. Choose carefully the type of business structure prior to spending any money. There are legal ramifications, tax considerations, paperwork requirements, and other considerations that can restrict your company's ability to react quickly to needed changes.

If you are going to take on a partner for your endeavor, make sure that you know this person very well, their abilities, etc and have clear communication regarding what your individual responsibilities will be. Choosing a partner without considering all of these facts will be disastrous. I went through some very tough struggles with a partner early on and it almost led me to stop the project completely. I found that the person I was wanting to go into business with was great at coming up with ideas, but when it came time to put in the time, effort and actual work to bring those ideas to fruition, the person was too busy with other areas of life to meet the obligation. This left me with an option of either stopping my project from moving forward or doing twice the amount of work I had initially planned. So, those of you who are looking to partner with someone, consider each others talents, ability to commit the time and effort to the project, and communicate well with each other. A partnership agreement is also very helpful. You should put into writing all the things you agree to, divisions of time, labor and contributions. Be sure to include remedies for disagreements or misconduct that will affect your company.

You should also give forethought to the type of products you plan to be offering. Some products are easier to make than others. Items such as whiskey and bourbon take great skill in order to make, however, these hard-to-make products can also be purchased on the open market from another distillery and re-branded as your own if you choose to go that route. Once you've decided on your first product, you will want to research and read as much as you can about it. It would be a good idea at this point to research names or even begin working towards graphic design of the label. Label requirements of the government are laid out in such a manner that by visiting the TTB (Tax and Trade Bureau) website, you can easily find everything you need regarding your label. Depending on the product you plan to make first, you may be required to submit a formula for approval prior to submitting your label for approval. All these things should be considered and planned for ahead of time so you do not find yourself a month or two behind simply waiting for label approval or for a formula approval. Obtaining a password from the TTB or Pay.gov can take time to be approved, so acquire it early. Approval to access online government sites such as formulation or COLA, for label approval, will also take time to process, expect delays.

Some things should be self-evident such as needing a bank account. A quick internet search will provide a variety of banks offering free business accounts and free checks. Many companies charge several hundred dollars for business checks, etc. I have saved hundreds of dollars in advertisement cost for banners, business cards, letterhead and other merchandising materials by price shopping on the internet. One of the favorite companies I have turned to has been Vistaprint. They always do a good job, are reasonably priced and ship quickly. I've resigned myself to writing this book as a general guideline as it would take volumes and volumes to detail everything you will encounter while starting your distillery. I trust you'll find this book useful as a guide to help you in the right direction to find the information you need, save you money and get underway. Throughout the book you will find mention of particular company names that I suggest as a resource. I received nothing in return for mentioning them and do so simply because I've been pleased with the service they provided me. There are certainly other companies out there and if any particular company thinks that they offer superior service or products that would be of use to a distillery, by all means, contact me and as revisions of this book come along. I will be happy to include them.

Are you ready to STAY committed to your idea, work through each and every problem? These are ideas and things that you MUST commit yourself to doing. Learn and accept there is NO room for quitting. You can expect to encounter problems, failures, lost and unrealized ideas along the way, but that's just part of it. You must keep progressing along and work hard. Become a person constantly looking to the future; stay thinking about 3 months ahead and keep track of daily, weekly and monthly operations. Being creative will help you immensely in seeking innovative approaches to problems. Don't give up; keep working until you find a solution. If plan "A" doesn't work, try an alternative. The end goal is the prize and it's a PROCESS getting there. The big picture can seem intimidating and monumental. If you break it into a series of small tasks, and accomplish one at a time, before you know it you'll be a distillery owner.

Chapter 2

Name, Location and Building

You would think that coming up with the business name would be easy to do. Naming your business is very important but can also be very difficult. People choose names for different reasons, to be a reflection of the company they hope to build for themselves, to represent their company persona, to be catchy or sound interesting. Whatever name you choose, keep in mind that it will be the public's association with your product and your distillery. You may want to give a lot of thought and make notes on the type of persona you want your company and product to have. In later chapters, I will get into branding and company persona more in depth, but from the outset you should be giving thought to whether your company will be a one of class and sophistication or one representing a creative flair and boldness. The name will suggest if your logo or designs should be refined, bold or subdued. Do an internet search for business name search engines where you can type in your proposed name to make sure it's not already in use. This will save you a headache in the future should you have naming issues or problems related to naming.

One of the biggest expenses you will incur will be your building. I will warn you now that renting or leasing a location is a bad idea unless you have a lot of money. As I researched before starting my distillery, I saw many case studies where companies were renting or leasing a location but due to the length of time it takes to open a distillery, the monthly drain on their savings by the lease and rent ultimately bankrupted their project before it could be completed. There are a lot of different ways you could go about finding a location for this type of business and ways you could make a lease or rent work for you, but for my company, the best move was to purchase a building at an inexpensive price. I began checking locations in cities nearby that were not economically thriving, as I knew that real estate would likely be less expensive there. I also looked for buildings that were in need of minor repair or upkeep, knowing I would be able to use that as a bargaining chip when negotiating the price of the building. For a micro-distillery your square footage will not be near as great as a full-scale distillery. Only you can determine the size of building that you will need based on your capacity, your future growth expectations and your volumetric considerations. You will also want to consider whether or not your location gives you room to expand because certainly you hope to grow at some point in the future.

Another consideration was to look for owner financed buildings. Owner financed buildings remove the costs that real estate agents usually charge both the buyer and the seller and you negotiate directly with the owner. In negotiating a price directly with the owner, a down payment is agreed on, a payment schedule is worked out for the length of the loan, and generally, this will be much less than renting or leasing a building. An example of this would be the property I came across in my area from various searches. I found the average lease or rent for the square footage building I needed to be anywhere from $1200-$1600 a month. I chose to purchase an owner financed building with a 10 year note. I paid $3000 down and the monthly notes are under $300. Additionally, I had a partner to split the cost with, which now brings the monthly note to $150 each, which is very affordable and will not drain our savings.

Before purchasing the building, contact the city and let them know the type of business you plan on putting in. You will want to make sure the area is zoned for your type of business and approved for alcohol related businesses. Many states have restrictions on the locations of alcohol related businesses. Federal requirements will also dictate how close to residences, schools and churches your business can be. All of these requirements can be found on the Alcohol, Tobacco & Firearms website or the TTB website within the Distilled Spirits Plant (DSP) packet for obtaining your permit. You will also want to check on the taxes of the property before committing to it. Be sure to check with the owner of the property to find out if you will be allowed to make interior changes as needed to support your business. Arrange to have the zoning officer check to make sure the business is up to code. Then you will be able to get your occupancy certificate as required in your area. Failing to check with the city or have zoning and inspection look at the building beforehand could be very costly to you. You could end up finding that the type of business you want to open cannot legally be opened at that location or that it would be too costly to bring the building up to code or that zoning precludes your business due to its geographic location or proximity to a school or a place of worship. Although this book may appear that I have you diving right into naming the business and looking for a business location you should not be at these steps until you have done a lot of research, reading, checking with state laws / federal laws and having some type of idea about requirements before you even begin. Other considerations which are building related will be its actual physical location. Do you have suitable parking and access for shipping that will surely take place at your location? Depending on where you live temperature could be a consideration in that your building would require heat or cooling. You should also consider if you will need standard electric outlets 110 V or 220 V and what is currently available in the building. You should also keep in mind that the federal government will require you to have a security plan on the building which means you must comply with the regulations to protect its contents or else they may determine that the building does not adequately protect their revenue and you will find yourself spending additional money to make sure the building is secure and built of substantial materials. For those of you that own property, there is a possibility you could build a building on property you already own if it is not precluded by law or zoning. But do not think that you will be allowed to start a micro-distillery in your garage or other structure that is attached to a dwelling or close to other dwellings. I have found that it is best to avoid these gray areas that would require a special visit or decision maker to pass judgment on, as it will only delay your process and waste your time if it is turned down. I would recommend getting on the internet and going to the Alcohol Tobacco and Firearms website and going through their menu to reach the Tax and Trade Bureau, (TTB) website, and reading the statutes and laws governing distilled spirits.

Do a general read of the law and highlight areas that you think will be important. You will find that you will refer back to this collection of laws again and again as you progress. The TTB website is full of information that will help you, so spend time looking through it and looking at the different forms and packets that are available for download. Once you get to the application process you will find that the government will want to know a lot about your location. They will inquire about the noise, waste, security, fire protection, storage capacity and energy use of your location. Another consideration is what you will have to do to the location you're looking at to make it usable for your purpose and acceptable by the city or county. If you are a very micro, micro-distillery, your fire protection requirements may not be too much. Your Fire Marshal or chief inspector may also require you to do a number of other things which could include installation of a sprinkler system, pull stations, sirens and horns inside and outside the building, all of which can be quite expensive. In my area a reasonable upgrade for a micro-distillery to meet the international fire code required spending $3-$4000 to add smoke alarms, heat sensors, a main controller box, warning sirens etc. before the building would be approved. But there are situations and areas where you could be required to have explosion-proof lighting, special electrical outlets, fire brick, heat resistant sheet rock or other fire protection. For these reasons it is important to have the fire marshal, city inspector or zoning look at the location before you purchase. By doing your homework and having a basic understanding of the requirements and checking with your local officials, you can choose a location that will fit your needs, cost little to prepare and leave you with a monthly payment that will not hurt. And that's what's really important isn't it? If you are able to pay your monthly mortgage easily from your employment without it interfering with your other obligations such as your living expenses, then it will be easy to maintain. Conversely, if the payment is large enough that it hurts and you find yourself struggling to pay your other obligations, then it will be difficult to maintain and very easy to come up with an excuse to end your project. So do not set yourself up for failure, instead, spend money and obligate yourself to financial requirements where they do not hurt and they will be easy for you to maintain and not become an excuse for you to back away from your project.

Chapter 3

Equipment

By the time you reach this chapter you may or may not have been on the TTB website and discovered that you cannot even turn in your application until you have purchased your building, your equipment, have it all in place and are ready to begin working. It was at this point that I began looking for equipment, pricing, comparing prices and began learning how to distill. Be warned, federal law states that it is illegal to distill without a permit. Some states allow people to make beer at home or wine at home, but federal law will not let you distill without a permit. You can search the Internet for distilleries that offer distilling courses, workshops or other training. The Original Texas Legend Distillery will offer short distilling workshops or even private lessons at a reasonable rate. A group class will likely cost under $500 most places and be well worth it. I can also recommend the great folks at Downslope Distillery, Andy and Mitch for a reasonably priced class. You may be able to volunteer your time working at a nearby distillery in exchange for gaining knowledge while there. You could also consider contacting a local micro-distillery and asking if for a small fee they would be willing to explain the basics of distilling to you and maybe giving you some hands-on experience under their watchful eye. I found some owners to be very cold and protective of their equipment to the point that they did not even want me to see it. I personally want to be of help to others. If time continues to allow, I will periodically put on workshops to teach others to distill or make myself available to assist in any way I can to help a person reach their goals even if they plan to be my competition. Competition will only bring better products to the marketplace and encourage companies to be efficient and selective of what they produce. I would always be open to doing a private internship providing our distillery has the time. In the back of this book I will list resources that I found for various types of equipment. Feel free to use them or locate your own. Do not be too quick to purchase equipment until you understand exactly what equipment you will need, its specifications and pricing options depending on where purchased. You will need to learn the terminology that is used in distilleries or exchangeable words to be sure that you are purchasing what you intend to purchase. Depending on the size of your distilled spirits plant, I can generalize the equipment you will need. Again you will need to refer to the statutes and regulations that govern equipment because the requirements do change depending on the size and capacity of the equipment you plan to buy. You will most likely find that you need at a minimum, one certified scale to weigh spirits. You will need to understand that this scale must be NIST certified and traceable. What does that mean? Get back to the internet and look it up. Yes, I could tell you everything, but you need to develop the habit now of researching and reading. There is a difference between equipment that is NIST certified and NIST traceable and you must make sure you are purchasing the correct one and that its capacity, increments of measure, and accuracy meet or exceed the statute requirements. The good thing is, the statute requirements are there for you to read and you can make sure that it complies before you make your purchase. You will find that you need hydrometers that measure specific gravity. These can be purchased at a local brew house frequently under $10 each. However, they will not meet the federal requirements unless they are certified and traceable. Once you begin looking for scientific equipment that is certified, traceable, that meet the increment requirements and range of measurement, you'll see that the prices will climb quickly. You can expect to pay between $100 and $180 per hydrometer and you are required to have several that meet specific requirements within the statute. You will also need specific thermometers not to mention the other equipment that is not specifically spelled out such as pumps, containers, pH meters, dissolved solids meters, various botanicals etc. You may choose to purchase your alcohol still or you may choose to build one. I would suggest a person read as much as they can on the art and science of distillation before making a decision on a still. The type of still and its size will affect its costs and its ability to perform the task that you need. Only you can answer the questions of how much volume you want to produce, type of liquor, space requirements in your building, so research carefully and make your purchase right the first time. You can visit blogs or forums for design plans or even builders that could construct your alcohol still for you. There are sites that sell commercial stills, sell used stills or have kits of various sizes. Choose carefully and make sure your purchase will fit your need and whatever you do, do not attempt to distill without a license. You will need other equipment depending on the type of alcohol you plan to produce. You will need a fermentation tank of one size or another depending upon the capacity in which you hope to produce. You may need other tanks or containers such as wash tanks, sparging, hot liquor, blending, finish or filter tanks. If

you're unfamiliar with any of those terms,
you should not be making a determination
about what you need to buy at this point.
There are a ton of books on how to distill
that cover terminology along the way. This
book focuses on how to start a distillery so I
won't be going into topics of distilling.
Research what those pieces of equipment are
and know for certain what you need before
you purchase and always compare prices to
see if you can get the same piece of
equipment elsewhere at a lower price. Some
equipment will be spelled out in the federal
statutes and regulations and give you clear
guidance on what criteria that particular
piece of equipment must meet. When the
law is specific, make sure that you comply
with the pieces you purchase. For example,
the law states clearly that the specific
gravity hydrometers required have a
particular measurement range and read in
particular increments of measurement.
These are absolutes. Although it also states
that a TTB inspector has the power to

approve any piece of equipment for use, you shouldn't risk your money on that approval. It's just easier to comply from the very start and buy what fits the criteria listed. Other items are not governed or mentioned specifically but you will need them nonetheless and that is why it is important to be familiar with distillation, storage and what is commonly in use or others have found to be useful. There are some plastics that are okay to use and do not impart flavors or off tastes. Some equipment will require hoses or clamps and you must make sure that you use ones that are suitable for drinking water and consumable products. Equipment needs vary so greatly and many can do two or three functions. It would be foolhardy to try to cover the combinations or the many uses within the confines of this book. In doing your research on the internet, blogs, forums and reading, you should be familiar with distillation its equipment. You should have a general feel for the expectations that are in the laws and statutes prior to making equipment purchases or choices on type. Another consideration when purchasing equipment has to do with size. The size of your building, volumes you expect to produce, and money that you have to spend in the purchase of those things. The only thing I could find in the law that relates to size generally said that the equipment must be of sufficient size for the person to conduct a profitable business. (Basically be large enough to be economically feasible that you can conduct business with it). If you plan to develop new recipes or combinations you will always have need for some smaller containers and smaller alcohol stills. To me it would make more financial sense to make your initial equipment purchases only large enough to meet those ends. That way if your project is derailed somewhere along the way to completion or you must stop prior to completion due to any reason; your losses will be minimal as compared to if you had purchased full-size equipment and a huge alcohol still. You can always purchase larger equipment later once you are selling product and still find use for your smaller equipment to develop recipes. You will also need packaging equipment, bottle filling equipment, labels, logo design and bottle tops. In the chapter on resources I will list the various places that you can obtain this equipment at reasonable prices. The more research that you do on suppliers and look for cheaper prices, the more money you will save. Keep in mind that the ideas that you have for design need to go beyond your personal taste. If you have the funds to do professional marketing you can determine what people find attractive in a name, bottle shape, catch phrase, slogan or color format; all of which are important for presentation of your product to the public. In this day of computers and Internet, you could use social networking to conduct your own marketing on a much smaller scale and you may be surprised to find that you need to alter your personal choice and make choices that are more appealing to the public in general. When purchasing some expendable goods such as bottles, buying in bulk is an expectation within the industry. If you plan to purchase less than an entire pallet of bottles you can expect to pay more per case in order to deal with a small amount. You may find a manufacturer that will sell you a couple of pallets and then be able to store them in a warehouse and ship them as you have room in your building depending on your storage square footage or you may be able to team up with a local winery to share the same bottle or for storage. You will need to ask if that bottle choice will be readily available, how long orders will take to be filled when you re-order and at what volumes of purchase do price breaks come. Some offer them cheaper if you buy more than the minimum order or you save money by the combined shipping of multiple pallets as opposed to multiple shipments of a single pallet. At every turn you will need to consider keeping costs low, meeting federal and state requirements and look for alternative ways to meet your company's needs such as pairing up with a local business or thinking outside the box to solve problems. Small commercial alcohol stills can cost anywhere from $30,000-$150,000 to purchase which can quickly exceed your budget. Instead, you may want to look on the Internet or brew supply stores for smaller equipment that would allow you to get started. One of my favorite sources for stills and equipment is Hillbilly Stills located in Kentucky. Some of the smaller alcohol still producers such as Hillbilly Stills make small versions that are very similar to commercial stills and are very affordable. I personally have used one of Mike Haney's Hillbilly Stills and found it to be easy to use, well built, affordable and produce a great product. To make things even better, Mike is just like you and I. He started with an idea, developed it, refined it, built it and then grew it. What more can you ask for? I have found supplies and equipment at various internet sites such as Brewhaus, Hot Sauce

Depot, various beer making and wine making supply stores, Revenoor, which are very useful and less expensive than commercial suppliers. You will need a lot of resources for all of your equipment and your expendable goods such as your base grains, yeasts, bottling supplies and equipment, and you should look for ways to obtain it at reduced cost or when you can, manufacture the equipment yourself to save money. Once your product is bottled and the topper placed on the bottle you will need some type of tamper resistant seal on the bottle. This could be in the form of a tamper resistant cap which you have purchased or you may choose to dip the top in wax to seal it or apply a plastic sleeve which you could use a heat gun to shrink and properly seal your bottle. You must think and give thought to every detail such as this to make sure that you have located a constant source of supply for every aspect so your production will not be interrupted by being unable to locate the supplies you need. Always research and check pricing at different companies to make sure that you are getting the best price on your sealing wax or shrink sleeves or bottle toppers that you can possibly get. Keep in mind that some of the equipment you purchase, the statutes and regulations require certification on and will ultimately have to be re-certified or you will have to purchase new certified equipment. Finding companies that can re-certify equipment or perform tasks like maintaining the certification on your fire extinguishers or fire system will be very important for you to keep on file so as not to interrupt your business. Your building and your equipment are going to be huge investments of your resources and I don't think it's possible for you to do too much research. Read as much as you can from books, blogs and the Internet and when you think you can't read anymore order some books on CD's and listen to them. These items are where you could spend the most money or with proper research save the most money.

Chapter 4

Persona and Feel

When you come up with a general idea and "look" that you want to portray in your product and company it will be important for you to maintain that persona or "feel" throughout all of the advertising, label designing and company persona that is publicly viewed. For instance, at The Original Texas Legend Distillery our company persona is that of the 1800s. As I developed this idea, I wanted to reach back to a time in my state that was legendary, when legendary figures such as Sam Houston, Davy Crockett, Stephen F Austin, the Alamo and tales of the old West that became legendary existed. We viewed this period as a time when legends were created and the people of this state largely relied on themselves and handcrafted the things that they needed. To stay true to that idea we determined that we would handcraft our product, personalize it by the person who crafted it as witnessed by the signature of the distiller on the back of every bottle and even in the development of our label we used motifs, style, and printing techniques that were less than perfect but would have been true had they been used in the time of the 1800s. All of these things played a part in the development of our company persona and our product image. Thinking along these lines should be a part of your creative process in determining the style you wish to portray your company and product to the public. Give some thought to your location, city, state, or what you hope to portray as you develop these things for your product and company. Even a vague idea can produce results by a person with creative talents. Do an Internet search for a company called 99 designs. This company has freelance graphic designers willing to help develop your logo or other graphic needs at very low prices. You basically will offer a set amount of money and the designers will look at the project you are suggesting and only those that wish to do that project will attempt to submit entries for you to judge. This process will ensure that designers that do submit entries, actively wanted to work on that project and are apt to be somewhat enticed or enthusiastic about the project they are working on. You will be required to pay the amount of money that you initially determined you would pay for the service to the designer whose project you choose. Early on you may want to establish a website or a social networking page that reflects your company's persona and the intended product you wish to make. Social media can allow the public or your targeted group to watch you grow, give you feedback as you progress and begin to become familiar with your branding and company persona. The support and feedback will at times be very encouraging and could potentially save you from making a mistake. When the feedback is not positive, you need to make a change in the direction or style that you chose. Utilizing social sites such as Facebook, MySpace, or twitter are all inexpensive ways to network to people who are future potential customers, potential suppliers, or others who are willing to help you market your product, supplies or express opinions which you will find useful. Early on when your advertising budget is small you may find sites such as Vistaprint.com as a great resource for items such as business cards, stationary, website hosting or other trivial advertising items at a very affordable cost. Friends and family can often provide suggestions or may even have talents that could help you such as web design or coming up with a catchy slogan. You will have decisions to make regarding printing labels yourself using standardized labels or having the labels professionally printed which can be very costly. Most expenditures encountered will need to be looked at and the data analyzed from several different angles. Does this item need to meet and have the ability to perform a particular function, is the item in compliance to statute and regulation, does the item need to reflect the company persona, is the item something that is renewable and will need to be replaced, is the item something that must be purchased from an outside resource or is it something that you are capable of handling in-house? If you ask yourself a broad range of questions regarding each expenditure and consider all things you will find that you make few mistakes in buying the wrong equipment, maintain true to your company persona, save money and stay within your budget.

Chapter 5

Permits

Licensing and permitting generally take between one year and a year and a half to complete. This reason alone is why it is important to make sure that your financial obligations are easy to meet and you do not run out of funds before you have even begun making a product. It is also crucial to time your purchase of particular equipment. Some equipment such as hydrometers should be bought late in the permit process and close to the time period that you will submit your application so that the certifications on that equipment will not lapse before you even get the opportunity to use them. The purchase of hydrometers, your scale, your fire extinguishers, anything that must be certified should be put off until right before you submit your federal application so that hopefully you will get your permits and be able to operate with the equipment and get some income generated before it is time to have that equipment re-certified. Your permitting process generally will begin with the federal application which can be found online. You must make sure that you fill out the DSP paperwork completely and exactly as the instructions tell you or else you are looking at having your application delayed. The federal government will not accept incomplete applications so it is not uncommon that an application be returned to you for corrections, resubmitted and possibly even returned again before the application is considered complete and is accepted. Part of the application process will also include the need for you to obtain a bond. You will need to obtain a bond that will cover your operations area of your building and also the unpaid tax of the product you produce. Since your individual needs will be dependent upon your equipment, volumes that you are making, and type of product, there is no way that I can make a bond amount determination for you. But again, if you do your research and check on blogs, forums, call and talk to some of the insurance and bonding companies that specifically deal with distiller's bonds you will get the information that you need to make an informed choice of what your initial bond amount should be. For instance if you obtain a bond for $60,000; 40,000 of that that bond may be to cover your operations area within your distillery and the remainder to cover the excise taxes of your product. Such a bond for a new company will likely cost around $1500 give or take depending on your individual circumstances. The bond form will take time as you must complete the federal form and have it notarized, then forward it to the bonding company with payment so that they may notarize it as well. And while I am speaking of getting the forms notarized, it would be a benefit to you to become friends with your local notary or have someone within your company become a notary as you will need many papers notarized for the federal application as well as the state application. Before starting a micro-distillery you may also want to check your state laws to see how the law addresses distribution of alcoholic beverages. Some states allow a manufacturer to self -sell their products directly to retailers, while others require the manufacturer to sell the product to the state and in those states, the state will make the sale to the retailer. Some states are also called three tier states. The three tiers are manufacturing, distribution and retail. An individual or company may only work in one of the three tiers and may not cross over into the other areas. Each of these types of distribution has their benefits and drawbacks for a micro-distillery owner. Texas as a three-tier state, requires that we sell our Troubadour Vodka, Bourbon or Blended Whiskey to a distributor at a reduced, discounted price which is sufficient for the distributor to then sell it to a retailer at a discount which allows the retailer to make a profit as well. In situations such as this, a manufacturer or distiller cannot determine what their final shelf price will be. Instead, we negotiate the wholesale price of our product to the distributor in such a manner to try to reach the target price we hope for once the product is on the retail shelf. We have to try to estimate how much the distributor will tack on to the price and how much the retailer will tack on to the price in order to try to estimate what the final shelf price will be. This may all sound like a lot to take in but it is very important in order to be able to start a micro-distillery on a small amount of savings. You must understand the processes forward and backward so you do not spend money unnecessarily or have the funds required to hire professional consultants. At this present time, for $5,000, I will travel to your location and spend two days at your location offering as much advice as I can. The most beneficial advice I could offer you would be how to efficiently and easily add product lines, along with recipes and finishing techniques to get you some quality products ready to go out your door and begin making you money. Many of the legal forms that you will need for establishing your business and conducting business along the way can be found free of charge on the internet or through companies such as LegalZoom.com. This does not replace having competent legal counsel but is a cost-effective alternative to the high cost of legal counsel. If you have an extra $1000 you may find a local attorney that practices general law you could have on retainer to assist you with legal questions, contracts, purchase of property and review of contracts with distributors when necessary. Some will tell you that you will need to file for trademark protection for your intellectual property which essentially is your branding, logo, company name or slogan. A trademark only gives apparent ownership, however it does not guarantee protection for any of your intellectual properties. Trademark law is often confusing, but you may not name the product similar enough to another named product that a consumer may be confused between the two or that you are unfairly able to gain notoriety. Development of your intellectual property and the use of it in the marketplace will have a start date that is traceable should you have a trademark issue come up. At such time, you would need a lawyer to assist you in protecting your trademark or defending alleged encroachment of your products on another trademark. If you live in a state that requires distribution through another company you have much work to do. Just as many people have differing views on giant companies such as Wal-Mart, the same holds true for distributors. Some feel that Wal-Mart brings goods close to small towns that would otherwise not have access to those goods because the local small stores did not have the wide variety of products. Others feel Wal-Mart put many small businesses out of business and both sides have legitimate debates. There are only a handful of large distributors across the United States and those large companies easily take over smaller distributors or push them out of business. Demand for your product or having a unique product is the easiest way to have one of the large distributors take interest in your company and products. If you're lucky enough to find a local small distributor you will be more likely to be able to get your product to the retailers, especially if you are in a three-tier state. Large distributors are large because they deal in large volumes and large sums of money, neither of which a start-up small micro-distillery has. So working on obtaining a distributor in such an area may take weeks or months, but the survival of your business depends on being able to get your product to the public and you cannot ignore this fact. Additionally, being active in the community and networking may help you obtain distribution.

Chapter 6

The Federal Application

A quick internet search for the Department of Alcohol, Tobacco and Firearms can quickly lead you to a massive amount of information that you will want to read regarding your federal application. You can download an entire packet that will contain every form that you will need to complete and probably a couple that don't apply. Included in the packet are instruction guides that may or may not be useful to you in completing the application. Since everyone will have a slightly different scenario, I feel that it would be a waste of time to try to go through every aspect of filling out your federal application. Currently, you can even do your application online which is even quicker and should certainly be considered. If at any time you become confused as to how to answer a question properly, how many copies are needed, or what part applies specifically to you, you can always call or e-mail TTB to ask your question prior to submitting your application. Taking time and being patient while completing the application on the front-end will be beneficial. Do not become disheartened if your application is returned and corrections are needed, this is a part of the process. If you are unsure of the corrections that are needed, be sure to call and get clarification. You can expect spending about a week or more to properly complete the federal application and gather all the documents needed. I encourage you to take your time on the application and clarify anything you're not sure of before leaving any blanks or filling it out improperly and turning it in.

Having your distillers bond is also something that will take some time to complete and will be necessary to go along with your federal application. Part of the application process will require that you obtain signatures from your local government to verify the location of your distillery meets all the guidelines within your city and county. Visiting your city or county planning office as well as the office that oversees code enforcement will be necessary so your building inspections and required fire systems are in place and signed off on prior to getting the final signatures from your local government. Every city or county typically has certain fire codes that they will want your building to comply with based on the operations you plan on conducting at that site. It will be very important to visit with them, have them come out, become familiar with your planned operations and let you know what updates must done to your building to meet their expectations as some of the requirements could be quite expensive. The square footage of your building and its location will have a lot to do with the type of fire system and the amount of ethanol you will be able to store at your location. Also keep in mind that as a byproduct of distilling, there is a fair amount of waste-water that will be sent to your local waste-water treatment facility.

Due to the variety of waste-water treatment plants, it is highly recommended that you visit with them ahead of time, so you understand what will be required of you before you begin your operations. It would be a good idea let them know you will be pulling all the ethanol from that water before sending it to them down the drain. They may require you to ensure the pH level is raised, which is easily accomplished using baking soda. They will likely require the temperature to be cooled off as well. Some areas have excellent city water systems. You can make use of that water for your mash and possibly your final blending of your product. However, in most cases, you will want to contact a water supplier that does their own reverse osmosis treatment and can provide water to you for around $.25 a gallon as opposed to a dollar a gallon for bottled water.

I mentioned water disposal in this chapter because there is a form where you state that you will comply with your areas regulations as it pertains to disposal of waste-water. Another by-product of distilling is the spent grain which is most frequently given away to be used as supplemental feed for cattle and pigs. The last time I checked, the federal government has approved distiller's grain as a supplement for feed.

Chapter 7

The State Application

Be sure to check with your state's alcohol regulatory agency for the paperwork necessary to establish a distillery in your state. Each state has different fees and requirements as it relates to your building's location, proximity to schools or churches and the necessary fees that will be associated with running your business. Most states will require that you first receive your federal application approval before applying for the state license or permit. In my state, the permit by the federal government was accepted by the state as meeting certain legal requirements for my state without having to re-qualify. An example of this in my state is the product label. Once the label has received federal approval through the COLA process, I had only to submit to the state the approved federal COLA and automatically received state approval for my label. As with the federal application, check with your alcohol regulatory agency on any questions you have or clarification you need when completing the application. Hopefully mistakes that need correcting will be few and the process will go smoothly. My state required me to get certain forms signed by our city and county officials. It was nothing to worry over, but it can feel overwhelming. Just remember that everything is a process and you must work through that process regardless of complexity or time.

Chapter 8

Sourcing Supplies, Secrets, Off and Running

When searching for a resource for bottles you can always search the internet. One of the companies I found is located in Mexico and their name is Vitro. Another is Mexcor and Universal Glass. If I've failed to mention any of the companies that supply equipment it is not to be seen as the companies are not good suppliers, but perhaps I simply have not come across them or used their products. Any companies that would like me to include their products or services as resources for any future versions of this book should feel free to send me your information, catalog, or samples. Check your local brew supply places for items such as yeast, small amounts of grain for experimenting with recipes, small bottle filling devices and small volumes of other supplies. Another source of equipment and supplies is St. Pat's located in Austin, Texas and available also online. Distillers often use equipment is also used by brewers and wineries, so don't forget when comparing prices to check brewing supply stores and winery suppliers. You will need stills and boilers, tanks and or drums, to buy or build a filtration device, bottles, caps, corks, or other toppers, and the list goes on and on depending on how much of your operation will be done by hand or that you will be automating.

As I've recommended from the beginning of this book, you will save a ton of money by doing your research, comparing prices, starting small, and up-sizing your equipment once you have money coming in. If distilling is completely new to you, you will need to research to know the type of still to purchase and the types of equipment you will need but you shouldn't spend money for an adviser or consultant when it is so easy to do research on your own to answer these questions. I would visit local Brewers, wineries or distilleries to see how they are laid out. If the owners are friendly enough, perhaps they will share some good information with you. Reading online blogs will be very helpful in knowing what equipment other distillers are using, types of pH meters, thermometers, hydrometers, scales, measuring devices, as well as general distilling knowledge and recipes. I CANNOT STRESS ENOUGH; YOU MUST READ EVERYTHING YOU CAN FIND!

Secrets

One of the first things I noticed as I looked at the size of some of the distilleries and stills they had was the fact their annual case sales seemed to far exceed the ability of the equipment they had. Without boring you with the long story behind this, I will simply say there are many that purchase alcohol; open market commodity ethanol, to use as a base of the product they are creating or to raise the alcohol by volume (ABV) of their mashes beyond what yeast will tolerate in order to increase output. There are some who have even been very successful buying bulk alcohol, simply adding water to bring the proof down to the bottling level, applying their own label and marketed the product. While in many ways it does make good business sense to do this if you can purchase alcohol less expensively than you can produce it and then utilize it as a base or in some cases depending on the product, simply rectify and go to bottling. Often times, these products will lack a unique character unless you modify it greatly to really make it your own. You will likely find only a few people willing to talk about this aspect of the alcohol industry, but if it is something you want to pursue, you could certainly search the internet for companies that sell bulk alcohol, neutral spirits or sometimes ready product. However if you have intention of utilizing these, you will need to make sure you have a lot of money to make the initial purchases and more often than not, you can produce ethanol utilizing a local source of starch such as corn, potatoes, rice or other grain and do so quite cheaply.

Off and Running

Once you have all your permits and have ran some small batches to develop your recipe, you need to continually look ahead at least four weeks to make sure you have ordered supplies you are exhausting. You also want to make sure you are starting processes early enough to not have them hold you up, such as waiting for label approval. Working with distributors can be a new experience if you're in a state that will require you to go through a wholesaler in order to move your product. Don't wait until the last minute to look into these if you are required to use them. As for tracking your supplies, it would benefit you greatly to create spreadsheets which track your usage of supplies, cost of the items, a quick reference sheet for reordering, temperature conversions for adjusting alcohol by volume based on temperature and conversion charts from metric to US measurement.

Remember in some states you will not even be able to set your final shelf price. If you find yourself in such an area it would be best for you to determine the cost you pay to produce a set volume of product plus the cost of total packaging and your operating expenses so you can break it all down to a dollar amount per bottle or case and determine how much you need per unit to make your business successful. In my state, I worked backwards from what I wanted my shelf price to be and negotiated a wholesale price with my distributor that allowed enough room for the distributor to add their profit, sell it to the retailer at a price low enough for the retailer to add their profit to what will ultimately become the shelf price for the consumer. I should stress that you should continue to read and become as familiar with the laws as possible to avoid serious problems should you inadvertently violate the law.

One of the great ways to learn about the industry and meet really good people is to join a trade organization. I personally would recommend joining one in your own local state if one is available. Many organizations also approach lawmakers so you can have input on the laws within your state that affect you. If you find yourself in a state without a trade organization, one of the best I know of is the American Distilling Institute, founded by Bill Owens. The ADI is a wealth of information and Bill is a great guy who is very involved in the craft distilling industry. If you're a very social person, then networking and making friends may be right up your alley. If you're not, I would suggest partnering up or hiring someone who will handle your interactions with the public to network your company and brand in as many places as possible to help your visibility.

Did we really start this distillery on less than $50,000? Yes, we really did and with the proper research and careful spending you can too. That's not to say you will be able to operate very long with the equipment you purchased at the onset, because we certainly found ourselves up-sizing and growing almost immediately. But when the rules of the game require you have all your equipment in your building and in place before you even apply for a permit it is prudent to purchase useful yet small and inexpensive items whenever you can.

Taxes

Learn that your products are seen by the government as revenue. Your production must remain in clearly marked areas in your distillery (bonded area) until they are removed taxed paid. My distillery pays the federal tax every two weeks to cover cases removed from bond and transferred (sold) to the distributor, who then pays the state taxes. It can take quite a bit of cash to pay taxes on products until you get paid, so plan accordingly. Keep a few thousand handy for this purpose.

I hope that this short book has provided at least some information you find useful and helps you find your way more clearly than the path was when I tried to follow those who went before me. I am happy to answer questions I can if you would like to contact me, but if the depth or number of questions is too extensive, I will try to point you in a good direction to solve your problem. I believe secrecy actually hurts our craft industry and by being open, sharing information, ideas and helping one another we can raise craft distilling to a level that has never been seen before. If you use

Facebook, search for The Original Texas legend Distillery or my name and send me a friend request as I feel a kinship towards others in this field. My distillery also has a Facebook group called "Friends of The Original Texas Legend Distillery" if you'd like to join us socially. My distillery uses a low cost web hosting site, yet it provides us with a web presence, introduces our products to the web world and allows potential customers to contact us. It didn't require hiring a web designer and like everything else, a little research goes a long way towards saving money. I'm sure you can see the theme of "do all you can do yourself." It serves two purposes: You save money and become very knowledgeable about every aspect of your business. You can visit our simple website at:

www.TheOriginalTexasLegendDistillery.com .

Chapter 9

Completing the Application

If you will go to the TTB website and download the Distilled Spirits Plant packet, I will walk you through completing most of the documents. Some of the items are easily understood and it's clear what information is being asked for. Others are more difficult to understand. Hopefully, this will help you through the process.

Beginning with the Registration of Distilled Spirits Plant, TTB F 5110.41:

1. Your first serial number will be indicated here as "1". If this form is returned to you for corrections, your next submission would be marked "2" and so on with each new version submitted.

2.   This is where your EIN number will go. This Federal Employer Identification Number is easy to obtain by doing a simple internet search on "obtaining an EIN number IRS". Or go to IRS.gov and search.

3.   Self-explanatory

4.   Date submitting

5.   Leave the Plant Number blank as this will be assigned to you.

6.   The address of your facility

7.   Will likely be blank as your business address is likely your plant address.

8.   Your Operations will likely be "Distiller" "Processor who", "Warehouseman" and "Bottles".

9.   Likely will be "Original Registration" or "corrections to Original Registration"

10.   This will be blank and supplied by TTB when processed.

10A. Number of Pages attached to Registration. 10B comes into use if submitting a correction and using some pages from the first submission and now have some new pages to attach. 10C will only apply if you have another business which will apply to this business.

11. Self-Explanatory

12. Title of person completing the registration, Example: CEO or Manager.

Your registration will require you to attach supplemental pages which you will have to title and write yourself. You will need each of these pages dated, numbered and have your business name at the top of the page.

The Statement of Bond and Permits form is where you describe the bond you secured, how much of the bond is devoted to operations and how much for covering product that sits in the tax unpaid area or product in transit.

The Statement of Daily Production Capacity is a written account of your stills, their size and an estimate of their daily max production capacity in proof gallons if operating 24 hours.

The Document of Signing Authority is a written statement of who is authorized to sign for the company. You can include mention of any documents you plan to send in that also grant signing authority to anyone in particular.

The Statement of Business Organization is where you list the type of business you've formed, sole proprietor, partnership, LLC, Corporation etc. with a breakdown of all partners and ownership percentages.

The Description of the Distilled Spirits Plant will be a lengthy written description of your building, such as providing measurements of rooms and what different areas are going to be used for. We included a drawn diagram, county plat map of the property and pictures. We also included the legal description of the property as obtained from the county tax office.

The List of Equipment page should have all stills, tanks and equipment, size and list of how it's labeled. All tanks and stills must be labeled on the equipment.

The Statement of Accounting Records will be a written statement where you input your business name, owner(s) names, and state that you understand the requirements for keeping records and that you will maintain all accounting records and file all required paperwork as required by law.

The Statement of Physical Security will be rather lengthy. You will describe in detail all ways you have provided for the security of the building and product. Be sure to mention all locks, alarm systems, key restrictions, patrols or guard companies. Describe in detail anything that helps provide security and safety for the building/property/product.

Your Statement of Production Procedure will describe, step by step, the production procedure for your product. Include all points of measurement, transporting product from one step to another and the means used to move it. Describe the mashing, production, processing and storage of the product.

A separate description of Storage Operations (warehouseman) will be required. You should describe how and where your product will be stored within the building, describe and identify labels of storage tanks or drums and the capacity they have.

You will have a Statement of Operations (Processor) which you will be confirming that you will be conducting bottling (if you will be), mention if you will be de-naturing alcohol or manufacturing "articles" other than beverage products. You will state that you will or will not be re-distilling, that you have read the laws and understand cases must be marked in a particular way that conforms to the law and that movement of finished product will be to a bonded area and not removed until taxes have been determined. You will also state if any other business will be conducted at the location of the DSP.

You will also be required to complete a document on Environmental Information where you will estimate your energy consumption and disposal of waste products. The TTB understands that you will be estimating since you aren't in operation yet, so do the best you can. Explain as best you can your individual plan to handle waste removal that may include municipal trash collection. This form is TTB F 5000.29. You will also complete a Water Quality form where you attest that you will not pollute any waterways and follow laws governing water.

As a distillery operator, you will immediately complete federal forms due monthly and state forms. Processing, Production, Storage and Excise Tax forms need to be completed the first month you are permitted so make sure you have looked at those forms, prepared to complete them and store copies of them. Most can now be done electronically but you will need password approval before you can submit them, so make sure you get those passwords for filing on www.Pay.gov BEFORE you actually need them. You'll need passwords for access to the federal label approval and formula submission online sites as well. These can take weeks to get, so again, apply for them now before you actually need them.

I hope you will let your creativity lead you in new directions and always progress in your effort to create a business. I really hope to see more micros launched and ultimately, band together to influence laws that govern our craft and benefit small business.

This should get you heading in the right direction, save you time, money and ease the burden of your journey. Best of luck and God bless.

Chapter 10

Some Resources

Misc Supplies

www.hotsaucedepot.com

www.discus.org

www.labx.com

Stills

www.hillbillystills.com

www.revenoor.com

www.milehidistilling.com

www.vendomecopper.com

Grains

www.honeyvillegrain.com

www.northernbrewer.com

www.50poundsack.com

www.morebeer.com

Bottles

www.mexcor.com

www.unipack.ca

**This book was intentionally written with general
information for individual needs, varying state laws,
and present difficulties in stating specifics. It should
provide enough direction if a person applies**

themselves, they can gain the knowledge needed to build a micro-distillery for under $50,000. Read, Research and read some more.

The things that are contained here should not be taken lightly. I learned these things through making mistakes, correcting issues, finding solutions and learning a better way of doing things. You get the benefit of my hindsight so you don't find yourself ready to submit your label for approval only to realize you need a password, which may take two weeks to obtain. You'll know that you need to get these things before you need them. Little hints of advice can save you big headaches and money if you take them for what they are worth. It was only after going through this process that I realized others could use a guide to help them so they can start their business using tried and true methods and save the cost of paying for advice when you only need a little direction. I respect the drive that encourages you and will tell you that you will be challenged. Do not give up. Work through it no matter what the obstacle. I believe in you and tell you that you can do this. Just read, adsorb as much as you can, listen to others, study everything you can find and before you know it, you'll be here. I hope you will help others, share information and band together rather than be adversarial. I thank you for your purchase of this book and for supporting the products from The Original Texas Legend Distillery.

ABOUT THE AUTHOR

Thomas, was born in 1968 in Pasadena, Texas. He was schooled in Deer Park and attended San Jacinto College, Sam Houston State University and South Texas College of Law. He spent much of his life working in the Criminal Justice/Law Enforcement field at the county, state and federal levels. He spent his last non-distilling years in oil refining and gasoline blending. Thomas, his partners, and The Original Texas Legend Distillery are strong supporters of U.S. Troops, past and present. Thomas enjoys creative endeavors and adventure seeking. One of his pursuits is travel and doing things he has not done before. He has worked as an editorial columnist, and served as a City Councilman as well as volunteered on various projects and committees. Thomas moved to the Beaumont area when working in the oil refining field and it was here that he began looking at the crude oil distillation process that resemble many of the processes in beverage distilling, that he began studying and learning about the art of refining beverage ethanol . Today, he currently calls Livingston home and enjoys visiting frequently in Colorado. When not busy working, he enjoys meeting his customers and retailers and many have become great friends. He is married and enjoys spending time with his wife Kaye, family and friends.

43470722R00051

Made in the USA
Lexington, KY
31 July 2015